TEN ROSY ROSES

For Russell—
My wild climbing rose
—J.G.

Text copyright © 1999 by Dee Michel & Guy Michel
Illustrations copyright © 1999 by Julia Gorton
Printed in the U.S.A. All rights reserved. http://www.harperchildrens.com
Library of Congress Cataloging-in-Publication Data   Merriam, Eve, date
Ten rosy roses / by Eve Merriam ; pictures by Julia Gorton   p.   cm.
Summary: Ten rosy roses stand in a line until, one by one, ten children
pick them.   ISBN 0-06-027887-0. — ISBN 0-06-027888-9 (lib. bdg.)
1. Counting-out rhymes.   2. Children's poetry, American.   [1. Counting.
2. Roses—Poetry.   3. American poetry.]   I. Gorton, Julia, ill.   II. Title.
PS3525.E639T46   1999   98-27473   811'.54[E]—dc21   CIP   AC
Designed by Julia Gorton
1 2 3 4 5 6 7 8 9 10
❖
First Edition

TEN ROSY ROSES

Eve Merriam
illustrations by Julia Gorton

HarperCollins*Publishers*

10

Ten rosy roses

standing in a line,

9

Jan picks one and
now there are nine.

8

Nine rosy roses near the garden gate,

Nina picks one and now there are eight.

Eight rosy roses, along comes Kevin,

he picks one and now there are seven.

7

Seven rosy roses by the wall of bricks,

Pam picks one and now there are six.

5

Six rosy roses beyond the honey hive,

Helen picks one and now there are five.

Five rosy roses at the schoolhouse door,

4

Kim picks one and now there are four.

Four rosy roses near the maple tree,

Amos picks one and now there are three.

Three rosy roses beneath a sky of blue,

Rachel picks one and now there are two.

Two rosy roses standing in the sun, the

0

twins take a turn and now there are none.